Original title:

The Wandering Trail

Author: Harrison Blake

ISBN HARDBACK: 978-9916-90-104-5

ISBN PAPERBACK: 978-9916-90-105-2

The Heart's Hidden Routes

In silence whispers a pathway,
To places where secrets dwell.
Beneath the trees, shadows play,
A story waiting to tell.

The soft breeze carries a tune,
Guiding dreams through the night.
With every step, hearts attune,
To stars that shine ever bright.

Echoing Footfalls

Footfalls whisper on the ground,
A dance of memories past.
Each heartbeat, a subtle sound,
In the moment, forever cast.

Through valleys deep and hills so high,
The echoes linger, never fade.
A testament to life, we try,
In every choice, a path is made.

In Search of Sacred Vistas

Mountains rise with grace divine,
Above the clouds, the eagle soars.
To capture beauty, a heart entwined,
In sacred spaces, nature roars.

The rivers twirl, a dance of life,
Underneath the old oak's shade.
In every moment, joy and strife,
A landscape of dreams is laid.

Tales of Forgotten Trails

Where footsteps fade, the stories lie,
In the rustle of leaves and stone.
Whispered secrets in the sky,
Of wandering souls who roam alone.

Through tangled woods, the path winds slow,
Where time forgot to turn its page.
With every corner, mysteries grow,
In silence, a heartfelt stage.

Vistas of Solitude

Above the hills, a quiet sigh,
Mountains meet the open sky.
Whispers of the breeze at play,
Time stands still, and dreams delay.

Echoed thoughts in silence dwell,
In this peace, my spirit swell.
Nature's canvas, vast and grand,
Here I find where I can stand.

Pathways of Reflection

Winding trails beneath the trees,
Softly rustling with the breeze.
Footsteps echo on the ground,
In each path, new truths are found.

Mirror of the soul so clear,
In each turn, the heart draws near.
Taking pause to breathe the air,
In this journey, none compare.

The Map Within

Lines etched deep upon the skin,
Stories waiting to begin.
Every scar, a tale to tell,
Inward journeys cast a spell.

Compass points to where I stand,
Navigating this vast land.
With each heartbeat, I will find,
The map within, forever kind.

In the Heart of the Woods

Deep beneath the ancient boughs,
Leaves whisper solemn, take a vow.
In the shadows, secrets lie,
Underneath the endless sky.

Footsteps soft on mossy ground,
In this realm, a truth profound.
Nature's arms embrace me tight,
In the woods, I find my light.

Shapes of the Wandering Heart

In shadows deep where dreams take flight,
A heart unbound, seeks out the light.
Each curve and line tells tales untold,
In whispers soft, the secrets unfold.

Through hills of gold and valleys wide,
The spirit roams, no need to hide.
With every step, a story spins,
In the dance of life, the journey begins.

A Tapestry of Trails

Threads of paths weave in the air,
Colors blend, a canvas rare.
With every road, a choice is made,
In the fabric of time, dreams never fade.

Mountains called, the rivers sung,
In every heart, adventure's young.
Each twist and turn, a vibrant hue,
Stitches of life lead me to you.

Crescendo of Echoes

In the hollow spaces where silence dwells,
Echoes of laughter, like distant bells.
Whispers of moments that linger long,
In the heart's melody, we find our song.

Resonating through the twilight air,
Memories dance, with stories to share.
Each beat a reminder of love we keep,
In the quiet night, our souls shall leap.

Uncharted Rhythms

Beats of nature, wild and free,
In every heartbeat, discovery.
Step beyond the known, embrace the chance,
In the wild unknown, life's vibrant dance.

Waves of sound in the still night,
Guiding the lost towards the light.
In every step, new paths arise,
With open hearts, we touch the skies.

The Call of Untold Stories

In shadows deep, where silence lies,
The whispers of the past arise.
Each tale a thread, a woven dream,
In twilight's glow, they softly gleam.

Voices echo through the night,
Carried forth by hopeful light.
Each heart holds secrets, rich and rare,
The call of stories fills the air.

Rustling Leaves and New Beginnings

The trees awaken, branches sway,
As autumn's chill begins to play.
Leaves rustle softly, colors blend,
Marking moments time won't lend.

A crisp new dawn, a brand new start,
In nature's hand, a beating heart.
With every breeze, dreams take their flight,
Embracing change in morning light.

A Solitary Expedition

Upon the path where few have trod,
I venture forth, beneath the nod
Of ancient trees, their wisdom vast,
Embracing silence, left the past.

The world feels vast, yet filled with peace,
In solitude, my thoughts increase.
Each step I take, a heartbeat strong,
In nature's arms, I find belong.

Trails of Wonder

In winding paths, where dreamers roam,
Each twist and turn brings hopes back home.
The whispering winds, a guiding sound,
In every corner, joy is found.

Mountains high and valleys low,
With every step, my spirit flows.
The world unfolds with tales to share,
As trails of wonder lead me there.

Navigating the Unseen Map

Beneath the stars, where shadows dwell,
Whispers guide, a silent spell.
Each path revealed, yet hidden still,
In the heart's quiet, we find our will.

With footsteps light, we tread the ground,
In every lost place, there's truth profound.
The compass spins, yet we stand still,
Trust the journey, respect the thrill.

Veils of mist obscure the way,
Yet hope ignites a brand new day.
Through stormy nights and sunlit lanes,
Our dreams persist, despite the pains.

Here in the dark, our spirits soar,
Charting the course, forevermore.
With every turn, a story unfolds,
In navigating life, we are bold.

The Soul’s Scenic Route

Winding paths through forests deep,
Where ancient secrets softly sleep.
The road may twist, the light may wane,
Yet beauty blooms from joy and pain.

Mountains rise, their peaks aglow,
While rivers murmur tales of woe.
Each bend reveals a view so rare,
In every breath, we find our prayer.

Beneath the sky, so vast and bright,
In fleeting moments, we find our light.
With open hearts, we wander free,
Embracing all that’s meant to be.

The journey's long, yet worth the ride,
With every tear, our spirits glide.
Through landscapes rich, our souls set sail,
On the scenic route, we shall prevail.

Horizons Unseen

Beyond the reach of dawn's first light,
The whispers of the stars take flight.
A path lies hidden, far away,
Where dreams and hopes await the day.

In twilight's glow, the colors blend,
A canvas where the skies extend.
With every step, a mystery,
Towards horizons yet to see.

Traces of Light and Shadow

In shadows deep, the secrets lie,
While shafts of light dance and sigh.
Between the dark and bright we tread,
Where whispers of the past are said.

A gentle breeze stirs the night air,
Carrying tales of love and care.
Each moment, fleeting, softly flows,
In the balance where life glows.

Landmarks of the Spirit

In the valley of silent dreams,
The spirit rises, flows like streams.
Within each heartbeat, stillness sings,
A map adorned with sacred things.

Through mountains high and rivers wide,
Our inner journeys coincide.
Each landmark marks a tale of old,
A treasure trove, a heart of gold.

Footprints in the Dew

As morning breaks, the world awakes,
With fragile steps that nature makes.
On blades of grass, a shimmer glows,
Like whispered secrets that nature knows.

In silence wrapped, the day begins,
With every breath, the journey spins.
Each footprint left, a sign of grace,
In morning's light, life's soft embrace.

Steps Through Time

Each step I take, a moment gone,
Echoes of laughter, whispers drawn.
Footprints fade on dusty trails,
Stories linger where silence prevails.

Shadows stretch in the golden light,
Memories woven in tapestry bright.
Time is a river, flowing fast,
Yet the heart holds tight to the past.

Moments collide, a web we weave,
In each heartbeat, new dreams conceive.
Pathways diverge but always return,
Through the flames of the past, we learn.

As stars align in the twilight sky,
I carry the echoes as I walk by.
With each breath, a history born,
Steps through time, forever worn.

The Call of Distant Horizons

Beyond the hills where the sun sets low,
A whisper stirs, an adventurous flow.
Winds carry tales from lands unknown,
The heart leaps forth in a daring tone.

Rivers reflect the colors of dreams,
In the distance, the horizon gleams.
Calling me forth with a song so sweet,
Each footfall echoes with passion’s beat.

Mountains loom like giants of old,
Guardians of secrets, both timid and bold.
The path awaits beneath endless skies,
As I chase the dawn, where freedom lies.

With courage ignited, I answer the cry,
For adventure awaits, and I long to fly.
The world unfolds in a glorious dance,
To the call of horizons, I surrender my chance.

Lost Among the Pines

In the forest deep, where whispers blend,
Beneath the pines, I seek to mend.
Leaves rustle softly, secrets held tight,
Nature's embrace, a comforting sight.

Sunbeams pierce through the canopy high,
Illuminating dreams that silently lie.
Footsteps echo on a carpet of green,
In the heart of the woods, where I've never been.

Branches sway gently, the wind's sweet sigh,
Voices of memories that linger nigh.
Lost among pines, I find my way,
In the solace of trees, my fears decay.

With every breath, I connect and unwind,
A symphony played, the heart intertwined.
Among ancient giants, I stand alone,
In their shadows embraced, I've finally grown.

A Soul's Inward Odyssey

In the quiet hours of night’s embrace,
A journey begins to a hidden place.
Deep within where shadows dwell,
I seek the truths that my heart can’t tell.

Reflections dance in the stillness deep,
Unlocking secrets my soul must keep.
With every heartbeat, I delve inside,
Where dreams and memories gently collide.

Questions linger like stars in the dark,
Illuminating paths where I must embark.
The whispers of wisdom echo and flow,
In this odyssey of the heart, I grow.

Through layers of fear, I peel away,
To find the light that guides my way.
With courage unfurling, I face the unknown,
In the inward journey, my spirit has grown.

Navigating the Wild Unknown

Beneath the canopy, whispers call,
Roots entangle, shadows fall.
Each step cautious, heart in hand,
In this realm, we make our stand.

Mapping dreams through tangled brush,
Where silence holds a gentle hush.
Stars emerge, a guiding light,
In the wild, we embrace the night.

The creek sings softly, truth unfolds,
Revealing tales that time beholds.
With every turn, a story waits,
In the wild, our spirit elates.

Pathways leading to the known,
In nature's arms, we find our own.
Each heartbeat echoes, wild and free,
Together, we weave our destiny.

Pathways Unfurled

In the morning light, trails invite,
Whispers of nature, pure delight.
Each pathway leads to realms untold,
Stories of the brave and bold.

Over hills and under trees,
Dancing with the softest breeze.
Winding roads where dreams ignite,
Guide us deeper into the night.

Footprints fade, but spirits rise,
Courage blooms under open skies.
With every turn, horizons shift,
In this journey, we find our gift.

Paths converge in harmony,
Together in this symphony.
With every heartbeat, we expand,
In this vast, enchanting land.

Shadows of Discovery

In silence deep, the shadows play,
Secrets hidden through the day.
With gentle steps, we chase the dusk,
In every heart, there's vibrant trust.

Through tangled vines and creeping fears,
We weave our way through laughter and tears.
Each shadow learned, a tale embraced,
In the mystery, our dreams are laced.

The forest breathes, a sacred space,
Millennia carved upon its face.
In the echoing depths, we find our way,
In the shadows, we learn to stay.

Together we rise, seeking the lost,
In every heartbeat, we count the cost.
With open eyes, and hearts so wide,
In the shadows, hope will guide.

Echoes in the Wilderness

In the vastness, echoes sing,
Nature's chorus, wild as spring.
Each sound a memory, soft and clear,
In the wilderness, we shed our fear.

Mountains loom with ancient grace,
Time weaves stories in every space.
Through rustling leaves and winds that sigh,
In their embrace, our spirits fly.

The river flows, a timeless song,
Guiding us where we belong.
In each ripple, a dream takes flight,
Illuminated by the silver light.

With open hearts, the wild we tread,
In echoes found, no words unsaid.
Together forged by earth and sky,
In this wilderness, we learn to fly.

A Walk with Shadows

In twilight's grasp, the shadows creep,
They whisper secrets, soft and deep.
Side by side, they dance and play,
Leading my heart on a winding way.

Through trees that sway, in muted light,
They guide my steps with gentle might.
Each path a story, each turn a dream,
In this quiet world, nothing's as it seems.

They flicker like thoughts in the fading sun,
A silent dialogue, two become one.
With every step, a tale unfolds,
Of fleeting moments, and memories told.

As night descends, the shadows grow,
A familiar comfort in the afterglow.
In their embrace, I find my peace,
A journey onward, a sweet release.

Labyrinthine Thoughts

In winding mazes of my mind,
Confusion lingers, hard to find.
Each twist and turn speaks of fear,
A silent echo that draws me near.

Conversing with ghosts of paths not taken,
Whispers of dreams that lie forsaken.
In shadows deep, clarity hides,
A world of wonder where chaos resides.

Fractured visions mirror the nights,
Fleeting glimpses of lost delights.
With every step, the questions grow,
Seeking answers the heart could know.

Yet in this maze, a spark remains,
A flicker of hope that joy can reign.
Through tangled thoughts, I may yet see,
The labyrinth's heart, a map to me.

The Spirit of Exploration

With every dawn, a world anew,
A call to venture, to break through.
Mountains rise and oceans gleam,
Awakening the explorer's dream.

The skies above, a canvas wide,
A promise of wonders, my constant guide.
Footsteps echo on paths unknown,
In every heartbeat, the seeds are sown.

Through vibrant forests, across the plains,
Chasing whispers like summer rains.
With spirit bold, I chart the wave,
For in this journey, the brave find brave.

A compass heart that seeks the stars,
To map the distance, erase the scars.
In every quest, a truth unfurls,
The beauty of life, the joy it whirls.

Embracing Nature's Whimsy

In fields where wildflowers sway,
Nature teases the pulse of day.
With laughter bright, the sun spills gold,
Embracing moments, tender and bold.

The breeze carries stories from afar,
Rustling leaves, a wandering star.
In every bloom, a fragrant sigh,
A gentle nudge to spread wings and fly.

Whimsical paths where the river flows,
Each twist a secret, each bend bestows.
In the dance of shadows, I lose my way,
Yet find sweet solace in the play.

With every heartbeat, I feel her call,
The earth beneath, the sky above all.
In nature's arms, I learn to roam,
Forever guided, forever home.

A Symphony of Sights

Colors dance in twilight's glow,
Nature's canvas steals the show.
Birds sing sweet in gentle breeze,
Whispers float through laughing trees.

Mountains rise with timeless grace,
Rivers carve a path, a trace.
Stars emerge in velvet night,
Dreams take flight in pure delight.

The Unfolding Path

Every step a new surprise,
Life reveals through dawnlit skies.
Footprints left in shifting sand,
Guiding thoughts to what we planned.

With each turn, new sights unfurl,
Every twist, a chance to twirl.
Heartbeats echo as we roam,
Finding purpose, finding home.

Reflections on the Journey

Moments linger, softly sway,
Memories that light the way.
Time weaves tales of joy and pain,
Lessons learned through loss and gain.

Glimmers of the past appear,
Whispers of what once was dear.
In the mirror, faces shine,
Each a thread in the design.

The Distance Beneath Our Feet

Earth beneath, a steady ground,
Roots immerse where life is found.
Mountains stand like dreams of stone,
Whispers of the paths they've known.

Feel the pulse of ancient lore,
Waves of time that crash and roar.
Through the soil, our essence thrives,
Connection deep, where life derives.

Where Shadows Dance

In twilight's glow, the whispers play,
Amidst the trees where night holds sway.
Figures twist where moonlight bends,
In every corner, magic sends.

The air is thick with secrets held,
In gentle night, the heart is quelled.
Soft echoes call in rustling leaves,
As daylight fades, the spirit weaves.

With every step, shadows entwine,
In this dim realm, the stars align.
Ghostly forms in every glance,
Here within, where shadows dance.

Amidst the dark, a spark ignites,
Illuminating hidden sights.
In every corner, life enchants,
In the stillness, shadows dance.

A Compass Without Directions

Lost upon a barren shore,
No guiding star, no settled score.
With no north, my heart adrift,
In endless waves, I seek a gift.

The sun sets slow, a fiery globe,
I wander through this azure robe.
Each step I take, the sand it sways,
In this vast void, my mind it plays.

Waves crash softly, memories swell,
In whispered tales, I find my spell.
Yet, with no map, my heart does roam,
In this wild sea, I seek a home.

A compass spins, but never finds,
In every heart, love's voice unwinds.
So onward do I drift along,
In silence wrapped, I hear the song.

Echoes Beneath the Canopy

Underneath the ancient trees,
Whispers weave through autumn's breeze.
As sunbeams dance on emerald beds,
Life's gentle pulse where silence treads.

Mossy floors, a fragrant maze,
Nature sings in subtle ways.
Beneath the boughs, time lingers slow,
In every shadow, secrets flow.

Birds converse in notes of gold,
Stories of the brave, the bold.
Eager roots grasp earth's embrace,
While hidden paths recall their grace.

In twilight's hush, I pause to hear,
Echoes soft, both far and near.
This sacred space, where spirits play,
Beneath the trees, life finds its way.

Secrets of the Untamed Path

A winding road through wildest lands,
Where nature's brush unveils its hands.
Each step reveals a tale untold,
In secret places, the heart behold.

Whispers of the wind align,
With every turn, the stars entwine.
Rugged trails and shadows roam,
In tangled thickets, I feel at home.

The scent of pine, the touch of dew,
Here, every path unfolds anew.
With every glance, the wild enthralls,
In whispered notes, adventure calls.

Step by step, I chase the dawn,
Where secrets of the earth are drawn.
Among the wild, my spirit thrives,
On untamed paths, my being drives.

Journeying to the Unknown

With every step, the path unfolds,
A whispering breeze, a tale retold.
The night sky glimmers with stars so bright,
Guiding the brave through the veil of night.

Mountains rise like giants bold,
Secrets in their hearts, yet untold.
Crossing rivers, deep and wide,
The spirit of adventure as our guide.

In shadows deep and valleys low,
We find the strength to dare and go.
For on this road, though we may roam,
We carry within our dreams of home.

Where the Earth Meets the Sky

In the dawn, where colors blend,
Horizons stretch, and dreams ascend.
Clouds caress the highest peaks,
Nature whispers, softly speaks.

The sun dips low, painting the ground,
Where earthy scents and hopes are found.
Between the soil and the azure hue,
Lies the magic, pure and true.

With every breath, the world expands,
A canvas brushed by unseen hands.
Together with the stars, we lie,
In wonder, where the earth meets sky.

The Dance of Dusty Boots

Upon the trail where echoes dwell,
Dusty boots cast a rhythmic spell.
With every stomp, a story flows,
Of mountains climbed and rivers rose.

The sun-kissed earth beneath my feet,
A steady heartbeat, wild and sweet.
A melody of journeys past,
With memories spun, each one a cast.

As twilight falls, the shadows play,
In the dance, I lose my way.
But in the whispers of the night,
My soul finds freedom, pure delight.

Embracing the Great Unknown

With courage held, we step outside,
Into the wild, where dreams abide.
The path is unclear, yet hearts ignite,
In the embrace of the starry night.

Treading softly on uncharted land,
The echoes of hope, a guiding hand.
Through tangled forests, we traverse bold,
Life’s secrets waiting to be told.

In every heartbeat, courage grows,
As adventure calls, the spirit knows.
Together we rise, to face the dawn,
Embracing the great unknown, we're drawn.

Footfalls in Faded Memory

In corridors of time we tread,
Echoes whisper, softly said.
Footsteps fade where shadows lie,
Painted dreams that never die.

Faded photographs, a silent ballet,
Dusty stories of yesterday.
Lingering scents in the air,
Fragments lost, yet always there.

Eyes that glimmer like stars at night,
Casting warmth in fading light.
Each memory a fleeting spark,
Guiding us through the dark.

Time may blur, but hearts recall,
The gentle rise, the bitter fall.
Embraced in moments, bittersweet,
Life's canvas, incomplete.

Terrain of the Soul

Mountains rise, valleys deep,
In silence, secrets keep.
Footprints mark the rugged trails,
Stories woven in the gales.

Rivers flow through endless lands,
Worn by time and gentle hands.
Echoes of a restless heart,
Searching paths, yet torn apart.

Sunset paints a golden hue,
Illuminating paths so true.
In the stillness, whispers bloom,
In shadows cast, we find our room.

Awakening in fields of grace,
Every turn, a warm embrace.
Terrain vast, yet deeply known,
Within our souls, forever sown.

Between Rocks and Reverie

Beneath the cliffs, the waters gleam,
Tales arise, a distant dream.
Whispers wander, secrets drift,
In the stillness, moments lift.

Pebbles shimmer, memories gleam,
Caught in tides of a timeless stream.
Glimmers of thought, softly tread,
Dreams are born where shadows led.

Between the stones, a world takes flight,
Guided by stars in the quiet night.
Breezes carry a tender tune,
Echoing sweetly, under the moon.

In reverie, hearts find their way,
Navigating the dusk of day.
Boundless realms, where spirits align,
In whispers soft, the stars combine.

Glimpses of Enigma

In the hush of dawn, a mystery stirs,
Hidden truths, like soft furs.
Glimpses flash in fleeting light,
Illuminating the silent night.

Curious whispers weave through the air,
Entangled thoughts, a subtle snare.
In shadows long, a riddle plays,
Chasing echoes through endless maze.

Each glance holds a secret in tow,
Fragments of what we might know.
The heart beats on, a puzzle unfolds,
In stories wrapped, yet untold.

With each breath, the enigma deepens,
Searching for answers, the soul beckons.
Yet in the chase, we often find,
The beauty lives in the undefined.

Heartbeats Along the Way

In twilight's hush, we wander slow,
With every step, our heartbeats grow.
The path ahead, a whispering sign,
Each moment shared, your hand in mine.

The stars above, they start to gleam,
Guiding our dreams like a gentle stream.
With every laugh, a memory blooms,
Together we dance under the moon's soft tunes.

In shadows deep, and sunlight bright,
We find our strength in shared delight.
Through valleys low and mountains high,
Our heartbeats echo, reaching the sky.

The journey's long, but joy we find,
Each winding road, our souls aligned.
With every heartbeat, we pave the way,
Together forever, come what may.

Of Trees and Tender Trails

Among the trees where whispers dwell,
The stories weave a secret spell.
Each leaf a tale of years gone by,
In dappled light, the shadows lie.

The trails we tread are soft and wide,
With nature's beauty as our guide.
In every rustling, a song we hear,
The pulse of earth, both close and near.

Beneath the boughs, we pause to breathe,
In quiet moments, we softly weave.
Connections deep, in silence found,
In tender trails, our spirits bound.

As seasons shift and branches sway,
We walk together along the way.
With hearts attuned to the gentle calls,
Of trees and trails, love never falls.

Timeless Labors of the Foot

Each step we take, the earth replies,
In graceful movements, under skies.
The journey sings with every stride,
In timeless labors, we abide.

With calloused soles and a dream in sight,
We chase the dawn, we seek the light.
In fields of gold, our paths converge,
As spirits high, we start to surge.

Through cobbled streets and rivers wide,
With faith as our unyielding guide.
Each labor brings a hidden grace,
In every footfall, we find our place.

The journey's end, a distant gleam,
Yet with each step, we build a dream.
In timeless labors, both bold and true,
The world unfolds, anew with you.

A Tread Between Two Worlds

In twilight's glow, the realms collide,
A tread between, where hearts confide.
With whispers soft from shadowed trees,
We find our dreams upon the breeze.

Two worlds await, both near and far,
In gentle steps, we follow stars.
Where magic stirs and wishes rise,
In the space between, our spirits fly.

Each choice we make, a dance of fate,
In every moment, we navigate.
With hands entwined, our fears dissolve,
In this tender tread, we both evolve.

The bridges built with love’s warm fire,
A journey fueled by deep desire.
In this passage, hand in hand we stay,
A tread between, come what may.

Serpentining Through Silence

In shadows deep, the whispers flow,
A winding path where few may go.
The trees stand tall, guardians old,
Their stories wrapped in silence bold.

Beneath the moon, the night winds sigh,
A gentle breath, a fleeting cry.
Each step a dance, a silent trance,
Where time stands still in night's expanse.

Among the leaves, the secrets weave,
A tapestry one can't conceive.
With every rustle, soft and low,
The heart beats on, in quiet throe.

Through dim-lit trails, the echoes flow,
A serpent's path, a sacred show.
In nature's breath, the silence blooms,
As night unravels, the soul resumes.

Illuminated By Starlight

Beneath a sky of twinkling dreams,
Where silver rays dance and shimmer gleams.
The universe whispers in gentle flight,
Stories unfurling, illuminated by starlight.

Each star a spark, a wish we send,
Guiding our hearts as they blend.
In cosmic arms, we find our place,
Inside the vast, eternal grace.

Galaxies swirl in a vibrant blend,
Creating paths that twist and bend.
In the quiet night, we breathe anew,
Bathed in starlight's endless hue.

The universe listens to every plea,
A dance of fate, wild and free.
With every twinkle, hope ignites,
Illuminated journeys, exploring heights.

Journey’s End and Revelations

At last, the road, now folding close,
The winding path, a wearied prose.
With lessons learned and tales untold,
In heart's embrace, the truth unfolds.

The sun dips low, the shadows play,
A final breath at close of day.
In quiet moments, wisdom flows,
Like rivers deep, where knowing grows.

We gather memories, a treasure trove,
Each moment cherished, love engraved.
As chapters close, new stories start,
In the silence, a beating heart.

Through every trial that we embraced,
The journey’s end is not misplaced.
For in each ending, life shall blend,
A cycle born, the stories mend.

The Unseen Guide

In gentle whispers, paths are drawn,
An unseen guide, through dusk and dawn.
With every step, a presence near,
A light that comforts, calms our fear.

Through winding roads, we navigate,
Trusting the winds that shape our fate.
With faith as compass, hearts aligned,
In unseen realms, our truths we find.

Each leaf that falls, each star that gleams,
The unseen guide fulfills our dreams.
In quiet moments, we feel their touch,
Reminding us we are loved so much.

Through life's wild dance, we roam and sway,
The unseen guide leads us on our way.
With grace and hope, they light the path,
In every trial, they share our path.

Between Echoes and Horizons

In twilight's hush, we linger near,
The whispers of dreams, crystal clear.
Over valleys vast, shadows play,
As night unfurls its velvet sway.

A dance of stars in endless flight,
Embracing the soft glow of night.
Between the echoes, our hearts collide,
Finding solace, where hopes abide.

The horizon beckons, a distant muse,
With every step, we gently choose.
Moments woven in twilight's seam,
We chase the remnants of a dream.

Lost in a canvas of muted hues,
Each brushstroke sings of faded blues.
Between echoes and horizons wide,
We're boundless souls, forever tied.

Wandering Without a Map

With compass lost and skies unmarked,
I roam where wild winds have sparked.
Through tangled woods and misty glades,
In search of paths that daylight fades.

Each step unplanned, yet heart so free,
Embracing the unknown's sweet decree.
In fields of gold and oceans deep,
The secrets of nature, ours to keep.

The journey calls, a siren's song,
Through meadows lush, where dreams belong.
Without a map, I carve my way,
In every shadow, night meets day.

And should I wander 'til I'm lost,
I'll cherish love, regardless of cost.
For adventure lies in the uncharted,
In fate's embrace, I am wholehearted.

Threads of Nature’s Lattice

In weaving whispers, nature binds,
The threads of life in gentle finds.
Winds carry tales from tree to tree,
In fabric rich, we find the key.

Each petal soft, each leaf a word,
In the silences, wisdom heard.
A tapestry of emerald dreams,
Where sunlight trickles, softly gleams.

Behold the dance of flora's grace,
In every corner, a sacred space.
Roots intertwine beneath the earth,
With every cycle, a heart rebirth.

Threads of nature in harmony,
We stitch our lives in unity.
In whispered breezes, we take flight,
A woven world, both dark and light.

Sunlit Detours

On sunlit paths where shadows play,
We wander freely, come what may.
With laughter bright, we trace the light,
In every step, the world feels right.

Detours taken, roads undefined,
Lead to treasures, joy intertwined.
Through forests thick, past rivers wide,
Our hearts align, our spirits glide.

With every twist, new wonders bloom,
In vibrant hues, dispelling gloom.
The sun's warm touch, a guiding hand,
In sandy shores or starlit land.

In moments brief but bold and sweet,
We gather memories, each heartbeat.
On sunlit detours, we embrace,
The beauty found in every place.

Footsteps on Forgotten Roads

In shadows fall the silent tracks,
Where whispers linger, time unpacks.
Each step a tale, a memory stirred,
Of journeys lost and dreams unheard.

The gravel crunches underfoot,
As faded signs my heart resolute.
Past trees that lean with trustful grace,
In every turn, I find my place.

With echoes soft, the past recalls,
The laughter and the silent calls.
In every stone, a secret sleeps,
On forgotten roads, my spirit leaps.

Through winding paths where silence reigns,
I seek the peace that still remains.
With every footstep, I behold
The stories whispered, brave and bold.

A Journey Through Mystery

Beneath the veil of twilight's glow,
A path of fog begins to flow.
Each step unveils a hidden sign,
In the silence, answers align.

The air is thick with secrets spun,
With shadows dance, the day is done.
I chase the moon, a silver thread,
Through realms where dreams and fears are wed.

In echoes soft, the whispers speak,
Of ancient tales, so wise, unique.
Through ruffled leaves, a story weaves,
In hearts of those who dare believe.

Discovery lies just ahead,
With every turn, I'm gently led.
In mystery's grasp, I find my way,
As night transforms to break of day.

Serendipity's Path

Along the trail where fortune smiles,
Each twist and turn brings joyful miles.
With unexpected sights in view,
Life's wonders bloom, vibrant and new.

A spark ignites in chance's glance,
As destinies align in dance.
The paths we tread, with open hearts,
Unveil the magic that life imparts.

In every stumble, a gift revealed,
In laughter shared, our wounds are healed.
We wander free, yet guided still,
On serendipity's gentle thrill.

With every step, the world expands,
In wondrous ways, by fate's own hands.
And through this journey, hand in hand,
We find the beauty in what's planned.

Lost Among the Pines

Deep in the woods where tall trees sigh,
A hidden realm beneath the sky.
With needles soft, the ground is dressed,
In quiet peace, my heart finds rest.

The fragrant whispers fill the air,
With stories woven everywhere.
Among the pines, I roam and dream,
In nature's hug, I find my theme.

The sunlight breaks through branches wide,
As shadows dance, my fears abide.
In this embrace of green and gold,
A sanctuary, warm and bold.

With every step, the forest breathes,
Embracing souls as nature weaves.
In this lost place, I'm free, I'm found,
Among the pines, my heart unbound.

Paths Less Traveled

In the woods where shadows lie,
Footsteps quiet, spirits nigh.
Beneath the boughs where whispers dwell,
Stories linger, tales to tell.

Unseen trails weave through the trees,
Carried softly by the breeze.
Each turn taken, moments spare,
In nature's arms, without a care.

Fleeting echoes mark the ground,
In each corner, peace is found.
A winding path, a gentle guide,
Upon this journey, hearts abide.

With every step our souls ignite,
The paths less traveled bring delight.
For in the woods, we come alive,
Embracing life, we learn to thrive.

Footprints in the Dust

On a road where few have tread,
Footprints linger, tales once said.
Dusty lanes and sunlit beams,
Mark the path of fading dreams.

Whispers carried by the wind,
Memories of places pinned.
Each step taken leaves a trace,
In the earth, a soft embrace.

Beneath the stars, the stories flow,
Guided by the moon's soft glow.
In the silence, spirits rest,
Footprints show we gave our best.

With each stride, the past unfolds,
A journey rich with tales retold.
In the dust, we leave our mark,
A testament, a vibrant spark.

Journey of the Forgotten

In shadows deep, the lost ones roam,
Seeking solace, far from home.
A journey marked by echoes faint,
Whispers of what life could paint.

Through valleys low and mountains high,
The forgotten souls learn to fly.
With every step, they reclaim the night,
In the dark, they find their light.

Old memories in the mist arise,
Like stars reflected in weary eyes.
To move ahead, they cast away
The chains of yesterday’s grey.

In every pause, there lies a chance,
To weave a new and vibrant dance.
Onward they tread, with hearts unchained,
The journey calls, their spirits gained.

Whispers of the Open Road

The open road, a siren's song,
Inviting wanderers to belong.
With every mile, a vision clear,
A world of wonders waiting near.

Beneath the sky, both wide and bright,
Each horizon a new delight.
The whistle of the wind's embrace,
Speaks of freedom, time, and place.

In the rearview, memories glow,
As every turn reveals a flow.
A tapestry of dreams unfurled,
Painting journeys across the world.

So let us wander, lose our way,
In the beauty of each day.
For on this path, our hearts will find,
The whispers that unite mankind.

Meandering Through Time

Winding rivers, soft and slow,
Whispers of the days we know.
Footsteps echo, past and near,
Memories shimmering, crystal clear.

Every moment, a fleeting glance,
Dancing shadows in a trance.
Time, a tapestry unwinds,
Binding heartstrings, life entwined.

Beneath the stars, we trace our fate,
Stories told, we celebrate.
A journey woven, threads of gold,
In the heart, our tales unfold.

With every turn, a lesson learned,
In the fire of dreams, we burned.
Through the ages, we will roam,
In the echoes, we find home.

Compass of Dreams

In the silence, secrets lie,
Underneath the vast sky.
North and south, we seek our way,
Guided by the light of day.

Waves of hope, they crash and roll,
In our hearts, the compass stole.
Turning tides, they mark our course,
With every dream, we find new force.

Stars aligning, fate takes flight,
In the darkness, we find light.
Holding close what we believe,
In our dreams, we dare to weave.

Through the storms, we set our sails,
Trusting winds, we'll tell our tales.
Past horizons, we will gleam,
Finding paths in every dream.

Beyond the Familiar Bend

Curved roads hide what's yet to see,
Mysteries call to you and me.
Every turn holds stories vast,
Waiting for the die to cast.

Sunset colors, deep and bright,
Leading us into the night.
Voices echo in the air,
Promises of destinies rare.

With each step, we leave the shore,
Venturing forth to seek and explore.
Beyond the bend, excitement brews,
A tapestry of vibrant hues.

In this journey, hand in hand,
We embrace the unknown land.
Beyond the familiar, our spirits soar,
In the heart of adventure, we yearn for more.

Nature’s Stepping Stones

Pebbled paths and gentle streams,
Nature whispers, fostering dreams.
Planting seeds where gardens grow,
In every leaf, a tale to know.

Mountains high, the valleys low,
Every step, a chance to flow.
Breezes carry songs unsung,
In the wild, we feel so young.

Fields of gold, beneath the sky,
Nature's canvas, oh so spry.
Embrace the wild, let spirits free,
In every moment, simply be.

Through the trees, a path we trace,
In harmony, we find our place.
Nature's stepping stones, so divine,
Lead us home, where hearts align.

Paths to Elysium

On golden trails where dreams do weave,
Whispers of hope in twilight breathe.
Every step, a gentle call,
Awakening souls, a journey for all.

Through fields of light, the heart may soar,
In peace and beauty, evermore.
Each path a story, a life to claim,
In Elysium's glow, we rise aflame.

A Tread in the Twilight

As sun dips low, the shadows dance,
Footsteps linger in twilight's trance.
A moment grasped, neither day nor night,
In this soft glow, all things feel right.

The stars awaken, the sky a shade,
Where dreams converge, and fears do fade.
A silent echo, the heart's soft beat,
In twilight's arms, we find our beat.

Beyond the Veil of Comfort

Beneath the surface, courage lies,
In comfort's grasp, the spirit cries.
To venture forth, to leap and roam,
Beyond the veil, we find our home.

With each new dawn, a chance to rise,
Embracing change, the heart complies.
In paths unknown, the truth reveals,
Beyond the veil, the soul conceals.

The Art of Getting Lost

In winding roads where secrets dwell,
The art of getting lost, a spell.
Each twist and turn, a mystery spun,
In chaos found, the race is won.

With every step away from the known,
In unfamiliar lands, we have grown.
To lose our way, to break the mold,
In getting lost, true life unfolds.

Nature's Wandering Hands

Gentle winds weave through the trees,
Caressing leaves with tender ease.
Mountains rise, and rivers flow,
Nature's hands, a graceful show.

Whispers dance across the glade,
Sunlight's touch, a soft cascade.
Flowers bloom in vibrant hue,
Nature's art, forever new.

Clouds drift by in skies so blue,
Painting dreams with golden view.
Cascading waterfalls rush down,
Nature’s hands wear water’s crown.

In every corner, life abounds,
In every heart, its magic sounds.
From soil deep to sky's vast span,
Nature's hands embrace the land.

When Horizons Collide

Where earth meets sky in twilight's glow,
Dreams take flight, and spirits flow.
The sun dips low, a fiery seam,
Since time began, we chase the dream.

Colors blend in a painter's sigh,
A canvas vast, where moments fly.
Clouds gather, secrets held in trust,
As day departs and stars combust.

Echoes of laughter mingled with night,
Stories shared in soft twilight.
Horizons stretch, a world so wide,
Together we stand, hearts open wide.

In the stillness, a promise made,
Each moment cherished, never to fade.
With every sunset, a new chance grows,
When horizons collide, the magic flows.

Through the Veins of Earth

Deep below, the earth does pulse,
Whispers echo, life convulse.
Roots intertwine in silent prayer,
Veins of earth, a bond so rare.

Rivers carve through ancient stone,
Tales of journeys they have grown.
Every droplet, a story spun,
Through the veins, life's work is done.

Mountains stand with watchful grace,
Guardians of time, eternal space.
Their shadows cast, a gentle sweep,
Through the earth, the heart's own beat.

In the soil where dreams take hold,
Whispers of the past, untold.
From seed to tree, the cycle starts,
Through the veins of earth, life imparts.

The Threads of the Journey

Woven tight in life's grand scheme,
Threads of fate, a vibrant dream.
Every twist, a tale unfolds,
A tapestry of stories told.

Paths diverge and converge again,
Connections form through joy and pain.
Each step taken, a moment blessed,
The journey's heart, a soulful quest.

In laughter shared and tears released,
Threads of courage, fears decreased.
Embracing change, we learn and grow,
In every thread, our spirits flow.

As we traverse this winding road,
Hand in hand, we share the load.
Through every chapter, one truth remains,
The threads of the journey weave our gains.

Reflections on Rustling Leaves

Whispers of autumn dance in the breeze,
Golden hues flutter, swaying with ease.
Beneath the branches, stories unfold,
Memories cherished, in silence, retold.

The ground is a canvas, painted in gold,
Nature's own secrets, quietly told.
Each leaf a reminder of moments once dear,
Crimson and amber, they vanish, yet near.

A symphony murmurs in shadows and light,
A rustling chorus bids farewell to the night.
Embracing the season, so fleeting and wise,
In every soft flutter, a promise arises.

Beneath the Starry Veil

Under the blanket of shimmering skies,
The cosmos unfolds, where mystery lies.
Gentle starlight, a kiss on the faces,
Dreams intertwine in celestial places.

Whispers of night, in the cool evening air,
Time seems suspended, free from all care.
Constellations twinkle, a guide through the dark,
With each twinkling light, a flickering spark.

The moon is our lantern, glowing so bright,
Leading us forward through the velvet night.
Beneath this vast canopy, hearts start to soar,
In the embrace of wonder, we seek to explore.

Embracing the Uncharted

Beyond the horizon, where dreams take their flight,
Lies a path unexplored, bathed in soft light.
Treading the waters of courage and fear,
Seeking the answers that whisper so near.

With every new step, the rhythm feels strange,
In the dance of the unknown, we learn to exchange.
The maps may be faded, yet we choose to roam,
Finding our way, creating a home.

Winds of adventure call out our names,
Inviting our spirits to play wild games.
In the rush of the wild, there's beauty untold,
Embracing the uncharted, our stories unfold.

Chasing the Gentle Breeze

A whisper of wind through the tall meadow grass,
Calls me to wander, to linger, to pass.
Softly it dances, inviting my soul,
Chasing the moments that make us feel whole.

With open arms stretched, I welcome the flight,
Through fields of adventure, from morning to night.
The laughter of nature sings sweetly along,
In the heart of the breeze, I find my own song.

Each rustle and murmur, a story to tell,
Of dreams that awaken, of wishes that dwell.
In the arms of this breeze, I discover my way,
Chasing the gentle, and longing to stay.

Alongside the Silent Stones

In shadows cast by ancient grace,
The silent stones hold tales in place.
Whispers weave through time's embrace,
As echoes dance in sacred space.

With every step on mossy ground,
Secrets lie, waiting to be found.
Roots entwined, their wisdom bound,
Nature's voice, a sacred sound.

The twilight glows in softest hues,
While evening stars unveil the clues.
In stillness, hear the world renew,
As dreams emerge like morning dew.

Alongside these stones, we stand,
With open hearts and open hands.
In quietude, we understand,
The pulse of life across the land.

Serpentine Passageways

Through winding paths the shadows glide,
In serpentine, the secrets hide.
Every turn, a choice to bide,
With heart as compass, souls as guide.

The trees entwine, a tapestry,
Of whispers lost in memory.
In thickets thick, we seek to see,
The way that leads us to be free.

With every step, the mist shall part,
Revealing treasures of the heart.
In labyrinthine art, we start,
To find the light within the dark.

Serpentine whispers call us near,
To trust in paths that disappear.
Embrace the twists without the fear,
For every journey holds us dear.

Beyond the Edge of the Known

Where horizons stretch to meet the sky,
And daring dreams are born to fly.
Beyond the edge, where shadows lie,
We seek the truths we can't deny.

With courage stitched in every seam,
We chase the threads of fading dreams.
In realms unseen, the heart redeems,
A tapestry of hope that beams.

Stars above us, ancient guide,
In night’s embrace, we find our stride.
Through valleys deep, we will not hide,
For in our souls, the light resides.

So step with me, let's take the leap,
Into the vast, where secrets keep.
Beyond the edge, the world does sweep,
Awakening the dreams we reap.

Emblems of Journeying Souls

In every heart, a map unfolds,
With stories etched, like threads of gold.
Emblems worn from tales retold,
Of journeying souls, brave and bold.

Across the lands, in windswept plains,
We search for joy, we learn from pains.
These emblems speak, like gentle rains,
Of life's sweet dance, its soft refrains.

As shadows stretch and daylight fades,
We gather strength from each escapade.
In unity, the bonds we've made,
Illuminate the paths we've laid.

So let us walk, hand in hand,
Across the sea and golden sand.
In every heartbeat, we expand,
Emblems of journeying souls, we stand.

Whispers of the Open Road

The road unwinds before my eyes,
With every turn, a sweet surprise.
Beneath the stars, I hear the call,
A journey's start, excitement's thrall.

Through fields so vast, where wild things roam,
Each mile embraced, it feels like home.
The wind's soft sigh carries my dreams,
In endless paths, where freedom gleams.

Footprints echo on the dust,
With every stride, I chase the gust.
A map unfolds, my heart's the guide,
Adventure waits on every side.

So take my hand, let's wander far,
Together beneath the evening star.
The whispers call, they urge me on,
To places new, from dusk till dawn.

In Search of Hidden Horizons

With every dawn, a brand new quest,
I chase the sun, I seek the west.
A glimmer far beyond the trees,
Adventure stirs upon the breeze.

Mountains rise like ancient kings,
Their majesty, the hope it brings.
Through valleys deep and rivers wide,
I wander forth, my heart my guide.

In shadows cast by silent pines,
The world unveils its secret signs.
I listen close, the whispers hum,
Of distant shores and beats of drum.

To search for horizons hidden well,
Where stories bloom and echoes swell.
With every step, the promise grows,
In search of lands the heart still knows.

The Wayward Breeze

The breeze blows soft, it knows my name,
It dances lightly, wild and tame.
Whispers of wanderlust it shares,
A call to roam, it always dares.

It sweeps through fields of golden grain,
Caresses hills and kisses rain.
From valley low to mountain high,
It lifts my spirit, lets it fly.

With every gust, a tale it spins,
Of far-off lands and timeless sins.
Through forests deep and oceans wide,
The wayward breeze will be my guide.

Embrace the wind, let joy take flight,
In whispered dreams, we chase the light.
With every breath, a promise blooms,
The wayward breeze, my heart consumes.

Secrets Beneath the Canopy

Beneath the leaves, the whispers sigh,
In shadows deep, the secrets lie.
The forest breathes, a living lore,
With tales of grace and ancient core.

Sunlight dances on emerald hues,
While creatures stir to share their views.
Each rustle holds a story's thread,
Of paths once walked by those long dead.

Ferns unfurl with secrets rare,
A world concealed, beyond compare.
In whispered breaths, the echoes share,
The wisdom found in nature's care.

So linger here, in sacred space,
Embrace the hush, the soft embrace.
For in this place, where time stands still,
The canopy shares its sacred thrill.

Soliloquy of the Open Air

The whispering winds softly play,
In the dance of leaves on a sunlit ray.
Clouds drift slowly, secrets to share,
A quiet moment, free from care.

Birds sing sweetly, soaring high,
Painting arcs in the endless sky.
Nature's breath, a canvas wide,
With open arms, the world does guide.

Beneath the boughs, shadows play,
A symphony blooms where children stay.
Every sigh of the gentle air,
Carries dreams beyond compare.

So let me linger in this space,
Eager heart, a slower pace.
The open air, my soul's delight,
A soliloquy of purest light.

Mystique of the Meandering

Winding paths through woods of green,
Secrets held where few have been.
Each turn a story waiting to tell,
In the heart of nature, all is well.

Creeks babble soft with tales of old,
Whispers of magic in hues of gold.
Footsteps wander, lost in thought,
In every shadow, treasures sought.

The sun is low, the sky ablaze,
Time slips gently in this haze.
Branches arch like arms that beckon,
In the woods, my spirit quickens.

With every step, the world expands,
Mystique swirls through nature's hands.
So onward I go, drawn to roam,
In the meandering path, I find my home.

Songs of Rustic Wanderlust

Fields stretch wide under open skies,
Each blade of grass, a lullaby.
The call of the wild, a siren's song,
In quiet corners, I feel I belong.

Rustling leaves, a gentle refrain,
Crisp autumn air, sweet with the rain.
Across the hills, horizons call,
In their embrace, I long to sprawl.

Footpaths winding through fragrant fields,
Nature’s bounty, a heart that yields.
Sunset painted in vibrant hues,
With every step, I chase the views.

Rustic dreams whisper my name,
In wanderlust, I feel no shame.
Life's melody plays through each land,
In the vastness, I make my stand.

Where the Compass Spins

In the wild where the compass spins,
Freedom lives, and adventure begins.
Every direction calls my name,
In the unknown, I find my flame.

Mountains rise, touching the sky,
With each ascent, I learn to fly.
Valleys echo with promise and grace,
In every turn, a new embrace.

Oceans whisper the tales of yore,
With every wave, I crave for more.
Stars map the journey through the night,
Guiding souls in a dance of light.

So let the compass lead me true,
Through wild terrains and skies so blue.
In the field of dreams, no end within,
The heart of wander, where the compass spins.

Milton Keynes UK
Ingram Content Group UK Ltd.
UKHW022006131124
451149UK00013B/1032

9 789916 901052